Business Continuity

Business Continuity
Playbook

Edited by
Dean Correia

Vision and concept by
Bob Hayes

Collective knowledge strategy and execution by
Kathleen Kotwica

AMSTERDAM • BOSTON • HEIDELBERG • LONDON
NEW YORK • OXFORD • PARIS • SAN DIEGO
SAN FRANCISCO • SINGAPORE • SYDNEY • TOKYO

Security
Executive Council

Elsevier
The Boulevard, Langford Lane, Kidlington, Oxford, OX5 1GB, UK
225 Wyman Street, Waltham, MA 02451, USA

British Library Cataloguing in Publication Data
A catalogue record for this book is available from the British Library

Library of Congress Cataloging-in-Publication Data
A catalog record for this book is available from the Library of Congress

ISBN: 978-0-12-411648-1

For more publications in the Elsevier Risk Management and Security Collection, visit our website at store.elsevier.com/SecurityExecutiveCouncil

This book has been manufactured using Print On Demand technology. Each copy is produced to order and is limited to black ink. The online version of this book will show color figures where appropriate.

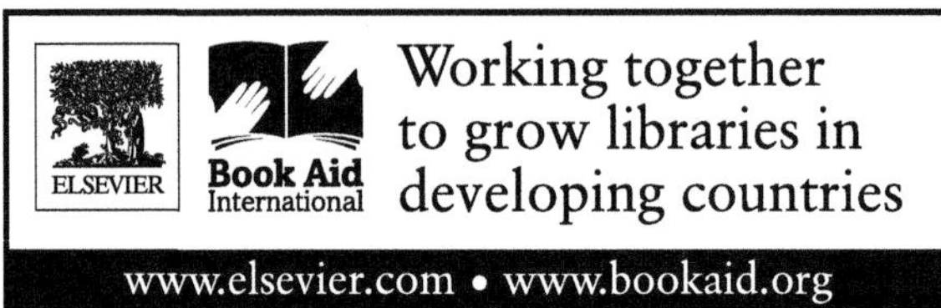

CONTENTS

Executive Summary ... vii

Foreword ... ix

What Is Business Continuity Planning, and Why Do I Need It? ... 1
The Value of a Business Continuity Program and its Services ... 1
Program Characteristics and Data ... 4

How Does a Business Continuity Program Help My Business, and How Is It Managed? ... 7
BCP Purpose, Principles, and Objective ... 7
Management of the BCP ... 9

How Do I Implement the Four Pillars of a Business Continuity Program? ... 13
Pillar I: Assessment ... 14
Pillar II: Preparedness ... 16
Pillar III: Response ... 20
Pillar IV: Recovery ... 25

How Do I Maintain a Business Continuity Program in the Long Term? ... 29

BCP Support and Annual Strategic Planning ... 29

Appendix 1: Specific Job Descriptions and Salary Ranges ... 31

Appendix 2: Advisory Committee Members ... 35

Appendix 3: Corporate Contingency Planning Umbrella ... 37

Appendix 4: Threat Risk Matrix and Heat Map ... 39

Appendix 5: Business Impact Analysis Template ... 41

Appendix 6: CMT/IMT/LRT Member List ... 51

Appendix 7: CMT, IMT, and LRT Member Roles and Responsibilities ... 53

Appendix 8: Crisis Management Meeting Locations and Contacts ... 63

Appendix 9: CMT/IMT Meeting Agenda ... 65

Appendix 10: Critical Incident Decision Matrix 69
Appendix 11: Critical Incident Individual Decision Matrix 71
Appendix 12: Facility Property Assessment Checklist 73
Appendix 13: Incident Report 75
Appendix 14: Government Contacts 77
References 79
About Contributing Editor Dean Correia 81
About the Authors 83
About Elsevier's Security Executive Council Risk Management Portfolio 85
Industry Applicability Validation 87

Executive Summary

The *Business Continuity* playbook provides a framework, tools, and checklists to create, manage, and execute all facets of an organization's business continuity program (BCP). In this playbook, the authors and contributing editor guide the security leader through development, implementation, and maintenance of a successful BCP. The text begins with a detailed description of the concept and value of business continuity planning, transitioning into a step-by-step guide to building or enhancing a BCP.

Security managers will understand and can immediately implement the four pillars of a BCP—assessment, preparedness, response, and recovery—using the instructions provided in the playbook. This playbook also explains how the security or business leader can maintain a successful BCP in the long term. Its 14 appendices, which include sample forms, templates, and definitions, make it an invaluable resource for business continuity planning.

WHAT IS A PLAYBOOK?

A playbook is an excellent tool for the security or business leader who wants to develop, implement, enhance, or validate a specific aspect of a security or risk management program. Playbooks provide a detailed treatment of a specific security program or service that can be quickly and effectively applied to an immediate need within an organization. Playbooks define and present the essential elements most often used by successful practitioners. They provide a framework that a security professional can use to set up, manage, and communicate the program to stakeholders. Playbooks also provide supplementary templates, forms, and checklists for immediate adaptation, and may be used by security professionals who need an introduction and plan for action on a new job responsibility, are adding a new program, or are validating an existing level of service. Playbooks are particularly useful for educators that are committed to providing current, relevant information and practices distilled from successful practitioners and programs and that have a direct correlation to current security positions.

Foreword

Business continuity planning is an activity performed daily by an organization to ensure that its critical business functions will be available to all respective internal and external stakeholders before, during, and after a crisis. The business continuity program is the tool that places that methodology into a structure to be followed by everyone in the organization in order to fulfill its business continuity planning requirements. Implementing a businesses continuity program has become a necessity for all businesses, regardless of size, and the benefits and return on investment a company will see when it does develop one are immediately measurable following a crisis or catastrophic event.

This playbook provides guidance to security and business leaders in order to assist with the creation of a business continuity program or enhance the program that is currently in existence. The material that follows has been compiled using various accredited sources, international standards, and the collective knowledge of the Security Executive Council (SEC) and its subject-matter experts, which represents decades of experience managing business continuity programs. It is adaptable to companies of all sizes from all industries.

Dean Correia
Contributing Editor and Security
Executive Council Emeritus Faculty

What Is Business Continuity Planning, and Why Do I Need It?

Business continuity planning identifies an organization's exposure to various risks while bringing together resources to provide effective assessment of, and preparedness for, those risks, as well as plans for response and recovery. Business continuity planning is an ongoing strategic practice governing how business is conducted. Long-term, fact-based, strategic business plans designed to attain the objectives of the business must be supported by parallel plans intended to ensure continuity of business operations regardless of the type of threat or risk encountered.

THE VALUE OF A BUSINESS CONTINUITY PROGRAM AND ITS SERVICES

Over the past few decades, business continuity planning has evolved from something undertaken by a few companies, primarily for compliance purposes, to a mission-critical part of every organization's annual strategic planning process. In an ever-changing global economy, companies are challenged to maintain their position as leaders in their industry. A requirement of maintaining leadership in the market is an understanding of various types and levels of risk. Business risks are unavoidable, quantifiable, foreseeable, manageable, and must be taken, especially by leaders.

Today's marketplace contains ever-present risks to people, assets, and brand, therefore all companies have a clear need to establish and execute a comprehensive **business continuity program (BCP).** If challenged with a critical incident, a BCP equips a company with the tools needed to respond in the quickest and most effective way possible for their employees, customers, business, brand, and external stakeholders. In order to effectively utilize the principles and best practices discussed in this playbook, it is critical for today's security leader to evaluate the current state of his or her organization's BCP (if one exists) or the overall readiness of his or her organization for a BCP (if one does not exist). In order to achieve the successful development, execution, and maintenance of a BCP, the security leader should determine why the organization needs to improve upon or implement a BCP.

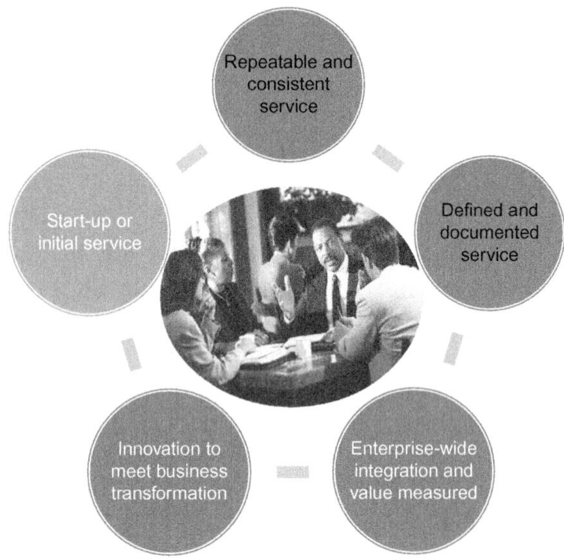

Use this diagram to assess the current state of your organization's BCP.

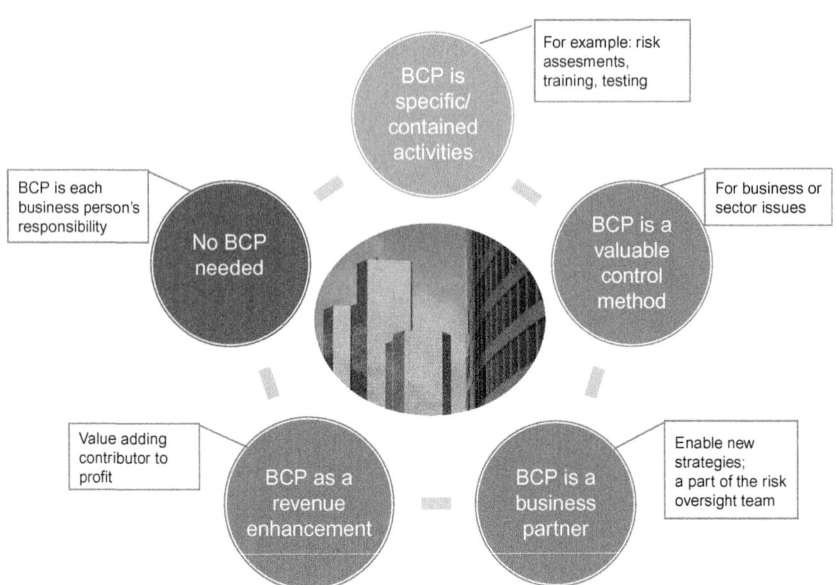

Use this diagram to assess your organization's overall readiness for a BCP.

When performing this evaluation, the security leader should ask himself or herself the following three questions:

1. **What role does business continuity have in my organization today?**
2. **Does this role match the current needs of the business?**
3. **What is needed to bridge the gap between the current role of business continuity and the needs of the business?**

As today's security leader, how do you show value, both qualitatively and quantitatively, for the program? Why not start by asking your leadership team the questions that business continuity planning often answers: "What if a catastrophic incident affects our organization?" "Will we be able to return to business quickly enough to avoid losing revenue or destroying brand reputation?" The most effective "what-if" scenarios should demonstrate how a plausible incident may disrupt operations specific to your business. Consider the following scenarios as examples to be customized to align with your organization's top risks, particular business environment, and strategic goals.

- **A major storm causes flooding and regional power outages, preventing a supplier from delivering components necessary for the manufacturing of your top-grossing product line. What options do you have?**
- **The local news is reporting that one of your company's products is responsible for the death of a local resident. How will you react to ensure that employee, consumer, and vendor confidence is maintained in your brand?**
- **An earthquake causes employees to spill out into the streets. Can you account for everyone? What do you do if employees need to address issues at home or later are afraid to go back into the building?**
- **Computer hackers install malware that destroys crucial plant equipment. Production stops until the equipment can be replaced. Is mass replacement of the equipment even possible?**

In "The Definitive Guide to Business Continuity Planning," Gregory Livingston notes that when terrorists first set off explosives at the World Trade Center in 1993, approximately 44% of businesses ceased operations at least temporarily due to the resulting fires.[1] He goes on to state that close to half of the businesses affected by the fires did not reopen. Some businesses learned from this event and implemented robust business continuity plans. Following 9/11, those businesses with effective business continuity plans fared better than those that did not. Livingston points to studies that have shown that, depending on the industry, one hour of downtime can cost a business up to $1,000,000/hour.

When considering your "what-if" scenarios, give thought to ways of quantifying the cost of the disruption to the business. Some examples are:

- Penalties or legal expenses
- Employee productivity lost or salary paid for unproductive work
- Brand damage leading to lost customers or increased staffing costs
- Direct losses such as ruined merchandise or lost sales
- Stock price declines or inability to finance debt at expected rates

As American basketball coach and player John Wooden once said, "Failure to prepare is preparing to fail." Can your organization afford not to plan?

PROGRAM CHARACTERISTICS AND DATA

Part of the value of business continuity planning for an organization comes as a result of its nimble, strategic nature if performed well. The program will allow an organization to:

- proactively identify and monitor emerging continuity risks;
- create and develop strategies to mitigate the impact of these key risks that are well documented and transferrable to all business units;
- facilitate security leadership having access to executive leadership support;
- develop and maintain a positive correlation between drivers and success in areas such as compliance, asset safeguarding, and brand protection.

According to original research from the Security Executive Council[2] and the 2008 Continuity Insights and KPMG Advisory Services Business Continuity Management Benchmarking Report,[3] researchers found that:

- 58% of business functions are considered mission-critical;
- The majority of companies targeted a recovery time of less than 24 hours. This varies widely by industry from four hours recovery time to more than 72 hours;
- Nearly 60% of organizations only plan for their longest outage to be seven days;

- 63% of BCPs have been around three years or longer;
- 74% of companies list government regulation and/or industry standard as a primary motivation for implementing their BCP;
- 72% of companies use BCP exercises to measure and communicate the impact and value of services to the executive level of the organization;
- 67% of companies have a senior management advisory or steering committee that provides input and assistance in the preparation, implementation, evaluation, and revision of the BCP;
- 40% of BCP coordinators have a C-Level title (i.e., the "chief" level of executives in a company, i.e., above director, chief risk officer (CRO), chief security officer (CSO), chief operating officer (COO), chief information officer (CIO), etc.)

In late 2009, Angus Reid Strategies was commissioned by American Express Small Business Services to conduct a survey of over 500 Canadian small businesses on (among others) the topic of business continuity. The survey results, published in the American Express Small Business Monitor, revealed some disconcerting news about the perception of business continuity planning and the overall lack of preparations made for a substantial, disruptive event. According to a *Bloomberg* news report,[4] "the majority of Canadian small business owners are unprepared to deal with common disruptions that can impact their ability to do business... [and] almost half of small business owners are unfamiliar with the practice of business continuity planning." It became apparent from this survey that small businesses are particularly vulnerable to prolonged business disruption in the event of a crisis because they have less time and resources to develop a robust business continuity plan.

Not only did the majority of Canadian small businesses feel too financially- and time-strapped to develop a BCP, it seemed that they also failed to understand the potential impact of what small changes they could make with minimal cost or effort. Seventy-five percent of respondents had not yet initiated any conversation whatsoever with their employees about what they can do to help restore normal business operation in the case of a crisis event. As recalled in the *Bloomberg* report, "one respondent from Quebec admitted that if several members of his team are affected by seasonal flu or H1N1, he can do little more than 'try to pick up the slack.'" This data reflects the need for education and training in the area of business continuity planning and the emerging importance of adopting a BCP for a company of any size.

How Does a Business Continuity Program Help My Business, and How Is It Managed?

In this section, a detailed framework to help security leaders build or enhance their business continuity programs (BCP) is provided. The purpose, key principles, and objective of a successful BCP are described, along with instructions for who manages a BCP. The steps in this section are adaptable to companies of all sizes and industries.

BCP PURPOSE, PRINCIPLES, AND OBJECTIVE

Purpose

The main purpose of a BCP is to enhance the protection of people and assets during a crisis while expediting the resumption of normal operations. The BCP addresses four main elements: assessment, preparedness, response, and recovery.*

Key Principles

The following key principles will underpin a successful BCP:

- **People Commitment:** The safety, well-being, and morale of the company's people and their neighbors along with the company's commitment to the common good are the key priorities of a strong BCP. The resourcefulness and dedication of the company's people and all of their internal and external process partners are the primary sources of information, methods, and application for these plans.
- **Total Quality:** Continuous process improvement and "critical-path" process identification, standardization, and management will produce plans that are invariably current, relevant, and quick and flexible to deploy. This also involves impeccable records management and documentation of all BCP activity.

*The four main elements or "pillars" of a business continuity plan are drawn from "Z1600-08: Emergency Management and Business Continuity Programs,"[5] and ASIS' "Business Continuity Guideline: A Practical Approach for Emergency Preparedness, Crisis Management, and Disaster Recovery."[6]

- **Growth and Innovation:** Through innovative, cost-effective planning, the revenue growth of the corporate enterprise can be economically protected and preserved.
- **Customer Satisfaction:** The BCP seeks to preserve the reputation of the company for integrity, honor, and trustworthiness and to maintain continuity of service and supply of products regardless of circumstances or events.

Objective

The company's objective is to protect and maintain the company's good name and reputation through the effective strategic and tactical management of all major incidents affecting the business, acting at all times to protect the well-being of employees, customers, vendors, and the community at large. In order to accomplish this, the business continuity planning process must perform the following 10 steps for planning a successful BCP.

10 Steps for Planning a Successful BCP

1. Identify key internal and external stakeholders that must be involved in the plan.
2. Identify any standards and legislation that sets requirements for BCP planning, records management, and review and build those requirements into the planning process.
3. Indicate the primary tasks to be accomplished by each stakeholder and standardize formats for consistency.
4. Identify tools and resources, from within and outside the company, needed to complete these tasks.
5. Prepare a list of the required materials for use in plan preparation at each level, both to initiate an original plan from which to build at each business unit and location and to compile consistent information at the major business unit and corporate levels. This information will assist in conducting risk analyses and in preparing the overall corporate plan.
6. Conduct a complete business impact analysis (BIA) throughout the entire company and its components in conjunction with plan preparation.
7. Inform, train, and educate all involved stakeholders in their responsibilities under the BCP and the resources available to them. Seek constant input and feedback.

8. Test and evaluate each component plan.
9. Continuously improve and update the plan at all levels.
10. Continuously inform all participants of changes that affect them; conduct ongoing training, drills, tests, and rehearsals.

MANAGEMENT OF THE BCP

Business continuity planning is an intricate process. Each element of the company is involved, from the board of directors to the managers of departments, suppliers, and strategic alliance partners. Therefore, while the details of the BCP structure may vary among organizations, any chosen framework should include top-level input from key stakeholders from across the organization. Senior management may designate a specific representative who, in addition to his or her other responsibilities, has defined roles, responsibilities, and authority for ensuring that a BCP is established, maintained, and reviewed in accordance with the BCP planning cycle (illustrated in the later section describing long-term BCP maintenance). This representative may hold the title of **manager, emergency preparedness/disaster recovery**. *(Note: Job descriptions for the manager, emergency preparedness/disaster recovery, and subordinate positions can be found in Appendix 1.)*

Led by the manager of emergency preparedness/disaster recovery (who may be alternatively titled management representative or BCP executive leader), an **advisory committee** should be created and include representation from functional subject-matter experts potentially impacted by identified hazards and threats. Other public/private stakeholders, vendors, and community representation may also be included. Accordingly, provisions are made for cross-sector representation on the committee. The individuals included in any one sector will depend on the size and complexity of the entity. The manager of emergency preparedness/disaster recovery has final authority in deciding the course of the program through its day-to-day administration; however, major decisions should be made in consultation with the advisory committee. Both parties should be in agreement concerning priorities and resource allocation in the day-to-day operation of the program. *(Note: A template to capture the names, functions, and contact numbers for advisory committee members can be found in Appendix 2.)*

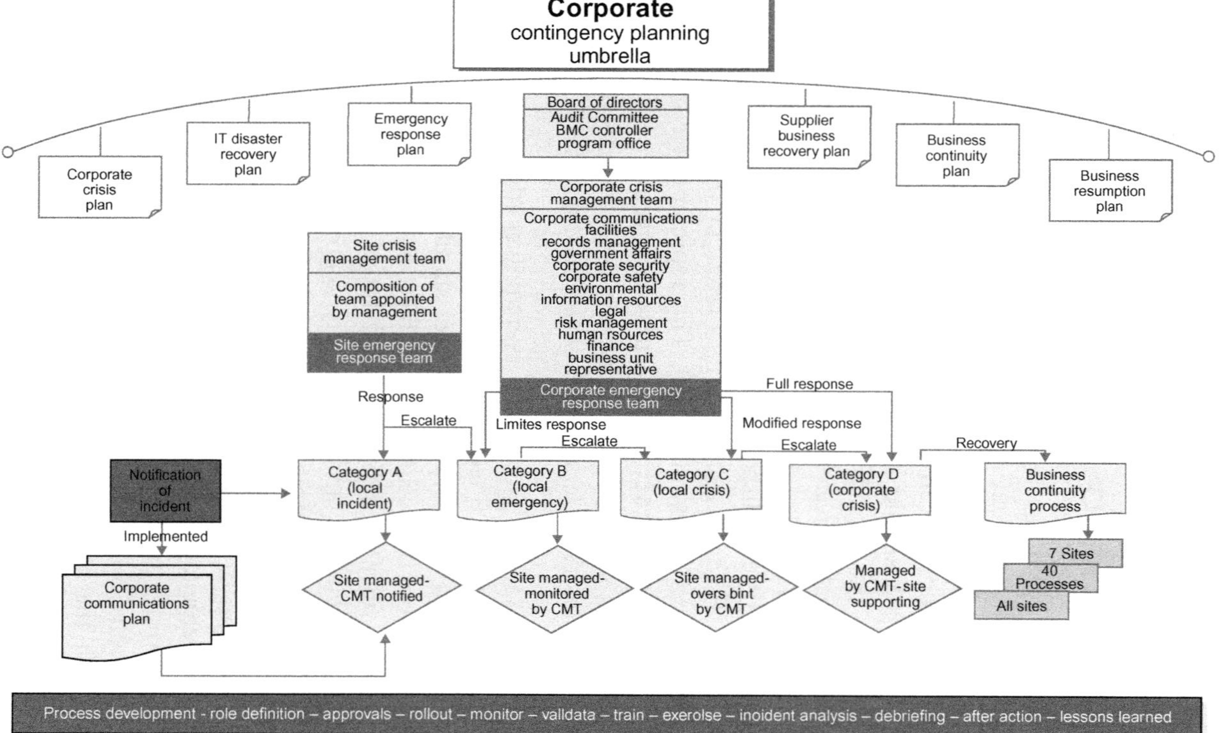

The corporate contingency planning umbrella.

The corporate contingency planning umbrella diagram illustrates a suggested framework for a company's BCP elements along with the interdependencies of **departmental BCPs**. The corporate BCP should strategically branch out as shown into specific departmental BCPs that cover **assessment, preparedness, response, and recovery** within their own areas of expertise. These four areas will be covered in depth in the following section.

How Do I Implement the Four Pillars of a Business Continuity Program?

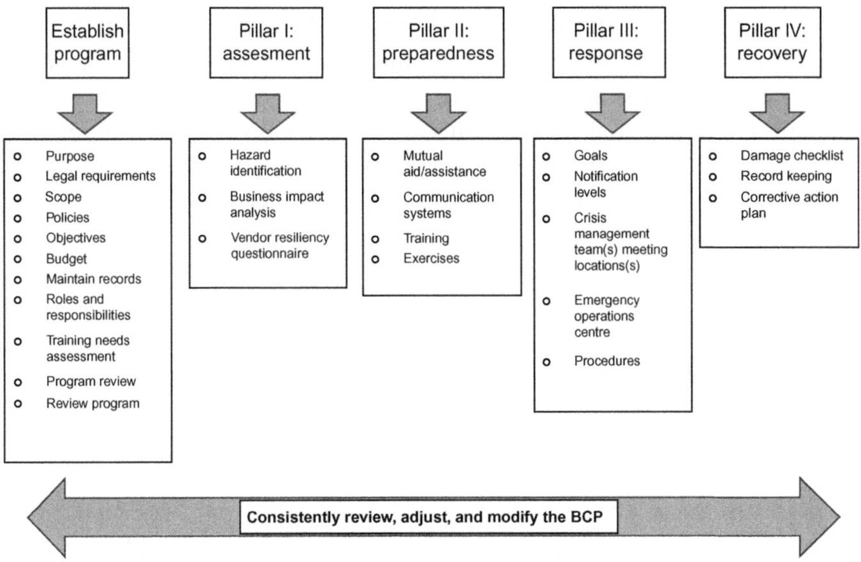

The four pillars of a successful business continuity program (BCP).

The figure above highlights the four interdependent risk-based functions of a BCP: **assessment** of business needs and risks, and **preparedness** for, **response** to, and **recovery** from emergencies. These functions can be undertaken sequentially or concurrently, and they are not independent of each other. This diagram can be used as a quick checklist for security leaders to compare what's currently in place in their organization and components of the plan that are missing. It will also benefit the security leader by its flexibility for customization specific to the current company personnel structure by illustrating who in the company should be involved, which components security exclusively runs, and when security should partner with other internal/external stakeholders.

PILLAR I: ASSESSMENT

Business disruptions can take many forms. Before a BCP can be developed to address these disruptions, one must understand what the risks to the organization are and how these risks might affect the business. This is the goal of the first core element of the BCP, known as the risk assessment.

Risk assessments should be conducted by a team of individuals who represent various business functions and support groups. As business plans change, risks and their possible effects on the business may change. Therefore, risk assessments need to be reviewed on a regular basis to ensure they remain relevant and effective. The assessment process should include hazard identification and risk evaluation. This information becomes the needs or requirements that the remainder of the BCP must address.

Hazard Identification

Hazards are typically grouped into three categories: natural (fire, flood, pandemic), human-caused (hazardous material spill or release, terrorism, fraud), and technological (software/hardware malfunction). Risk information should be gathered from all local, regional, and national industry, association, and governmental sources. During this process, keep in mind that threats and vulnerabilities can be internal or external to the business. For example, disruption to the business can be indirectly caused by crises suffered by suppliers, customers, the local community, or government.

Risk Evaluation

Not all risks are equal. Risks that are extremely improbable or that have little impact on the organization may need to be treated differently than high-cost events. Therefore, after identifying the hazards to the organization the next step is to determine the likelihood and possible impact of the events.

In order to effectively analyze and communicate the results of the assessments, they usually result in the construction of a threat matrix and heat map which show the relationship of risks to their probability and amount of damage to the organization. (*Note: Examples of a threat matrix and heat map can be found in Appendix 4.*)

Risk assessments should be conducted by a team of individuals who represent various company functions and support groups. The ASIS Business Continuity Guideline[6] recommends that when companies are performing a risk assessment, the company should keep the following four objectives in mind:

1. Identify internal and external threats and vulnerabilities
2. Identify the likelihood of an event arising from such threats or vulnerabilities
3. Define the critical functions necessary to continue an organization's operations
4. Define the controls in place or necessary to reduce exposure and evaluate the cost for such controls

Business Impact Analysis

To complete the risk assessment process, the probable impact of a threat or vulnerability on the organization must be determined. The process of determining and recording the extent and potential costs of business disruption is called a business impact analysis (BIA). The BIA will be used to develop recovery strategies and therefore needs to include enough information to support this task. (*Note: An example of a BIA template can be found in Appendix 5.)* According to the ASIS Business Continuity Guideline, the four major functions of the BIA are:

1. To identify critical processes
2. To assess impact if crisis were to happen
3. To determine maximum allowable outage and recovery time objectives
4. To identify the resources required for resumption and recovery

The identification and documentation of critical business processes should consider not only all business functions but also how they interrelate to each other. Allowable outage and recovery times should take into consideration seasonality. For example, longer outage recovery times may be acceptable during a time of the year where slower sales are expected. The resources required for recovery may include people, technology, data records, and third parties such as vendors or public sector personnel. When possible, the BIA should quantify the operational impacts in terms such as lost sales, increased expenses, regulatory fines, penalties, or other financial terms.

Vendor Resiliency Questionnaire

Most companies rely on outsourced vendors to support their operations in one or more areas. As these outsourced vendors are key members of a company's BCP, it is as important to assess their crisis readiness as it is the company's. This will provide the organization's leaders with a comfort level that the vendor is performing its diligence within the four pillars of the BCP to an acceptable minimum standard.

The company should establish a standard minimum score that the vendor must achieve in order to be deemed in compliance with the company's crisis readiness guidelines. If the vendor receives a failing score, it should be required to take remedial action within a designated timeframe in order to achieve the acceptable passing score and continue as an approved company vendor.

PILLAR II: PREPAREDNESS

The "Emergency Management Planning Guide 2010–2011,"[7] issued by Public Safety Canada, is an excellent resource for a discussion of preparedness and the purpose of preparatory training exercises. The guide states that "the objective of planning activities associated with preparedness is to have an effective and coordinated approach to BCP and operational readiness." The goals of planning activities related to preparedness, according to the guide, should include:

- Maintain a level of sustainable capacity, supplies, and resources to meet the goals outlined in departmental BCP plans that are based on priorities, needs analysis, and capability requirements
- Incorporate lessons learned and best practices into the BCP process for continuous improvement

As with other continuous improvement methodologies, the BCP will benefit from a continuous cycle of planning, implementation, testing, and improvement. Each iteration of the cycle provides learning opportunities that can be used to identify gaps or issues with the BCP. The opportunity for ongoing training this cycle provides ensures that all BCP team members, management, and employees are aware of and capable of carrying out their responsibilities in the BCP process.

Mutual Aid/Mutual Assistance

A mutual aid/mutual assistance agreement is any formal agreement between entities to share or provide resources, facilities, services, and other required support to one another during an incident. Examples include cooperative assistance agreements, service level agreements, and intergovernmental compacts. Such agreements may include neighboring or nearby private sector entities, as well as relevant government, private sector, and nongovernmental organizations. Mutual aid/mutual assistance agreements should be:

- developed in consultation with the parties involved,
- in writing,
- reviewed by legal counsel, and
- signed by responsible individuals.

At a minimum, a mutual aid/mutual assistance agreement should include the following elements or provisions:

- Definitions of key terms used in the agreement
- Roles and responsibilities of individual parties
- Procedures for requesting and providing assistance
- Procedures, authorities, and rules for payment, reimbursement, and allocation of costs
- Notification procedures
- Protocols for interoperable communications
- Relationships with other agreements among entities
- Employment standards/occupational health and safety/workers' compensation coverage
- Treatment of liability and immunity
- Recognition of qualifications and certifications

Communication Systems

Telecommunication and other communication systems should support all components of the program in order to notify and update key internal and external stakeholders regarding the incident. These systems can include the following:

- Traditional phone, wireless, and satellite telephones
- Pagers
- Fax machines
- Computer systems and networks, including personal digital assistants (PDAs), company intranet, external web sites

- Automated, purchased, or hosted systems and services that can simultaneously send and/or verify receipt of messages to telephone and computer devices
- Two-way radios operating on public, private, or amateur radio frequencies
- Public radio and television systems, including provision for interrupting broadcasts with emergency messages or superimposing messages on current programming
- Sirens and other outside warning devices
- Computerized incident management systems for sharing operational communications

Training

Individuals who perform tasks related to any aspect of the company's BCP are expected to be competent as a result of appropriate education, training, and experience. Training or instruction should be conducted at all levels of the organization, including C-level, and be specific to emergency management and business continuity duties and responsibilities as determined by a training needs assessment.

Training may be conducted through workshops, webinars, conference calls, internal or external courses, and industry-specific seminars. In the "Emergency Management Planning Guide 2010–2011," Public Safety Canada recommends that the training plan should address the following questions:

- What are the objectives of the training and what will it consist of?
- Who will be trained?
- Who will do the training?
- What training activities will be used?
- When and where will each session take place?
- How will the session(s) be evaluated and documented?

Exercises

An exercise provides the chance to simulate a real-world crisis. It promotes preparedness while offering the best opportunity to test the BCP and identify weaknesses. A simulation is a valuable way to improve the coordination and communication between various teams as well as judge the effectiveness of the training. It is crucial to involve all key stakeholders with involvement in the organization's crisis response plan.

Exercises can be designed to test certain portions of a plan or the entire plan(s). Some common exercise formats include:

- **Tabletop exercise:** A facilitator, who is not a member of the company's current crisis management, provides the group of attendees with details of a mock crisis scenario. Participants review and discuss the actions they would take in response to the scenario details presented by the facilitator. Specific response actions are not performed.
- **Functional exercise:** A facilitator, who is not a member of the company's current crisis management, provides the group of attendees with details of a mock crisis scenario. Participants perform some or all of the actions they would take in the event of plan activation to respond to the scenario. Specific response actions are taken.
- **Full operational exercise:** A facilitator, who is not a member of the company's current crisis management, provides the group of attendees with details of a mock crisis scenario. Participants suspend normal operation and activate the plans as if the event were real.

It is important to consider any applicable legislative requirements when determining exercise frequency and format. Exercises should be conducted when there have been significant changes to the business' key personnel responsible for implementing the plan or a new risk to the organization with a high probability of impact has emerged.

In order for an organization to realize a high degree of benefit from an exercise, the following best practices should be considered:

- The scenario should be as real as possible and be based on the risk assessment. This means that key stakeholders and resources, inside and outside the company, should be involved.
- Debriefing sessions should be included at the end of the exercise, with lessons learned documented.

PILLAR III: RESPONSE

A critical incident is a sudden, unplanned event that affects or potentially affects the company's ability to execute critical business functions and results in great damage or loss. A critical incident is characterized by:

- an interruption of normal business operations;
- the need for an immediate, coordinated response by numerous resources;
- and the potential to draw extensive news media and public attention on the organization.

The goals of critical incident response are to:

- protect human life,
- protect company assets and the surrounding community,
- contain the incident,
- communicate to all stakeholders and media,
- assess the effects of the critical incident, and
- decide on and implement optimal response plans.

Key principles in the management of all incidents include:

- initial assessment of the incident's impact,
- communication to involve stakeholders as deemed by initial assessment,
- continuous assessment, response, and communication updates to all internal and external stakeholders.

Important Crisis Management Skills

- Be calm—Crisis management requires clear thinking, emotional control, and balance.
- Be open-minded—Take in large quantities of information without tunnel vision and focus on listening.
- Be decisive—Decisiveness needs to be balanced with a willingness to consider ideas and input from others. Be willing to prioritize and make decisions with only partial knowledge.
- Be flexible—Adapt to rapidly changing situations. Remember that some information relayed about critical incidents is incorrect or incomplete.
- Be persuasive—Crisis management requires the ability to convince others to follow directions.

Response Teams and Expectations

Three interrelated teams may manage incident response at different levels within the organization.

1. **Crisis Management Team (CMT)**—The CMT manages the uppermost level of incident response, providing senior executive guidance and making decisions regarding policy, procedure, and finances as they relate to the management of critical incidents. The CMT may be led by the functional leader of a company's security department and should include executive-level representation. Other relevant external stakeholders may be brought in to support the CMT as required.
2. **Incident Management Team (IMT)**—The IMT actively manages critical incidents that extensively threaten employees, assets, and brand reputation from the corporate office. This group consists of subject-matter experts (SMEs) from each critical business function and may be led by a leader within the company's security department. Other relevant external stakeholders may be brought in to support the IMT as required.
3. **Local Response Team (LRT)**—The LRT responds to local critical incidents that extensively threaten employees, assets, and brand reputation. This group consists of local SMEs from each critical business function and may be led by the local leader of a company's security department. Other relevant external stakeholders may be brought in to support the LRT as required.

Members of the CMT, IMT, and LRT must:

- Attend training, exercises, and meetings as required (or send backups when necessary).
- Be knowledgeable in the four pillars of the company's BCP and review it at least quarterly.
- Keep the BCP with them at all times.
- Ensure that their designated backups are aware of their roles.
- Provide functional expertise as required during crisis management meetings.

(Note: A template to capture the names, functions, and contact numbers for CMT, IMT, and LRT primary and backup members can be found in Appendix 6. CMT, IMT, and LRT members and lead roles and responsibilities can be found in Appendix 7.)

Incident Notification and Escalation

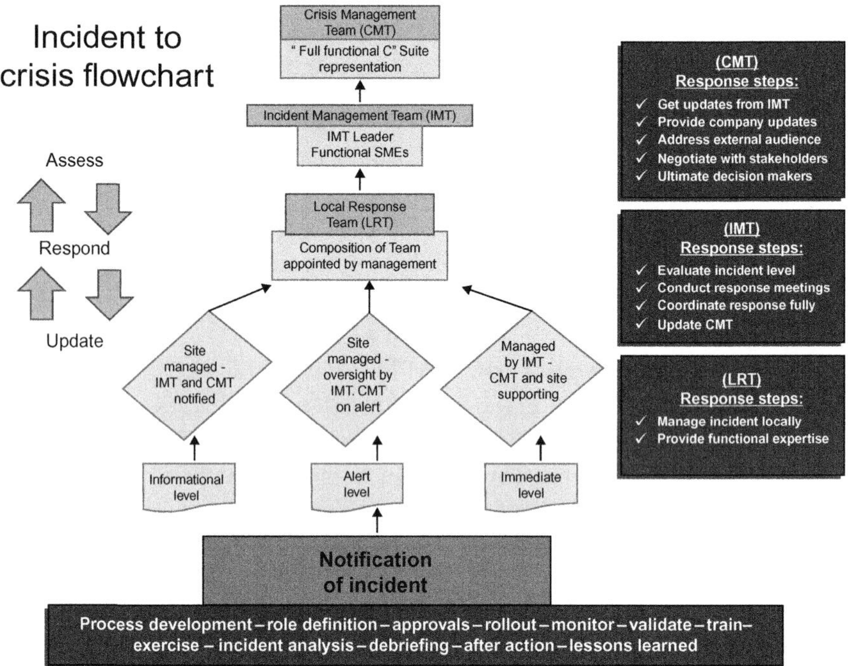

Incident to crisis flowchart, including the roles of each response team.

The diagram above illustrates the typical framework of incident management along with the interdependencies of all stakeholders. Regardless of the level of the incident, the IMT lead notifies the CMT lead of an emerging critical incident. Based on the incident's severity, the CMT lead determines when it is appropriate to communicate to respective CMT members at one of the three levels, which each include steps that should be followed.

Information Level

1. The CMT lead is contacted by the IMT lead regarding the incident. The CMT lead then contacts the remaining CMT members regarding the critical incident on a convenient basis, usually during working hours. The incident does not require a call to action.
2. The IMT meets in order to manage the incident. The IMT lead is responsible for tracking the incident status and updating the CMT

lead as necessary, who in turn updates the other CMT members accordingly.

3. If the incident is at a local level impacting people, assets, or brand, the LRT lead is responsible for alerting the IMT lead.

Alert Level

1. The CMT lead is contacted by the IMT lead regarding the incident. The CMT lead contacts the remaining CMT members regarding the critical incident regardless of the time of day.
2. The CMT lead contacts the other CMT members to establish representation and availability in the event that the situation escalates and a meeting is required.
3. Additional key internal and external stakeholders are identified and placed on call if the situation escalates.
4. The IMT meets in order to manage the incident from the corporate office level. The IMT lead is responsible for tracking the incident status and updating the CMT lead as necessary, who in turn updates the other CMT members accordingly.
5. If the incident is at a local level impacting people, assets, or brand, the LRT lead is responsible for alerting the IMT lead. The LRT meets.

Immediate Level

1. The CMT lead is contacted by the IMT lead regarding the incident. The CMT lead then contacts the remaining CMT members regarding the critical incident regardless of the time of day.
2. The CMT lead contacts the other CMT members to establish representation and availability.
3. Upon activation, respective CMT members will meet at one of these predesignated sites described below.
4. The IMT meets in order to manage the incident from the corporate office level. The IMT lead is responsible for tracking the incident status and updating the CMT lead as necessary, who in turn updates the other CMT members accordingly.
5. If the incident is at a local level impacting people, assets, or brand, the LRT lead is responsible for alerting the IMT lead. The LRT meets.

Crisis Management Meeting Locations

The CMT, IMT, and LRT should have clearly defined locations at which to meet and manage an incident. Some basic requirements of a primary and secondary meeting locations are the following:

- They are equidistant in opposite directions of the corporate office/ key facility.
- There are sufficient tables, chairs, and meeting supplies for the team members.
- An extra copy of the company's BCP is secured there.
- There is ample parking.
- The site has redundant power, Internet, television, and telephone capability.
- The site is accessible 24/7.

(Note: A form for documenting the locations of crisis management meetings as well as critical phone numbers and contact information is provided in Appendix 8.)

Emergency Operations Center

An emergency operations center (EOC) is a room or facility staffed by personnel charged with commanding, controlling, and coordinating the use of resources and personnel in response to a crisis. This room may be located at the corporate office. The EOC must be available to use 24/7 to monitor emerging risks to the company and may also be used to support the management of a crisis. The EOC should have similar features to the CMT meeting locations mentioned above.

Response Procedures

When an incident occurs at the local level, the IMT lead will need to initiate an update from the LRT lead to determine the following:

- What information is confirmed and what is unconfirmed?
- What decisions have already been made?
- Does a decision on any portion of the emergency need to be made immediately?
- What are timelines for pending items?
- Who is impacted?
- Are any employees, customers, vendors, or members of the community still in danger?
- Are any employee emergency contacts arriving on site? Who will meet the emergency contacts and where will they be taken?

- Is the incident area now secure?
- If needed, can ingress and egress be controlled?
- Is additional security needed?
- What confirmed damage has occurred?
- Has anyone spoken to the media? What was said and to whom?
- Has a site spokesperson been established?
- Is there a need for an immediate media statement?

Subsequent to the primary collection of information, CMT, IMT, and LRT meetings may be held to assess, update, and respond accordingly to the incident during the response and recovery. In order to maximize the efficiency and effectiveness of the meeting, an agenda outline should be used when managing the crisis. (*Note: Examples of a CMT/IMT and an LRT meeting agenda are shown in Appendix 9.)* Meetings also serve to collect and disseminate information and to support the determination and prioritization of action steps. (*Note: Examples of a critical incident decision matrix and a critical incident individual decision matrix are shown in Appendices 10 and 11.)*

PILLAR IV: RECOVERY

Once the extent of damage is known, the process recovery needs should be prioritized and a schedule for resumption needs to be determined and documented. The prioritization should take into account the fundamental criticality of the process and other factors, including relationships to other processes, critical schedules, and regulatory requirements, as identified in the BIA. Decisions regarding prioritization of processes should be documented and recorded, including the date, time, and justification for the decisions.

Once the processes to be restored have been prioritized, the recovery work can begin. The resumption of these processes may occur at either the current worksite or an alternate worksite, depending on the circumstances of the crisis. A facility property damage checklist is an effective tool to provide documentation of the damage suffered and how recovery should be prioritized. (*Note: An example of a facility property damage checklist is shown in Appendix 12.)* As the critical processes resume, the resumption of the remaining processes can be addressed. Where possible, decisions about the prioritization of these processes should be thoroughly documented in advance, as should the timing of actual resumption.

Postincident Recovery and Record Keeping

The company's employees are encouraged to follow the instructions below once authorities have reported that the area is safe and has been cleared for reentry. If possible, obtain written evidence of this authorization.

- Attempt to secure the site. If you are not able to complete this task alone, contact your manager and use your best judgment.
- If the site cannot be secured, consult with management regarding the removal of high-value items from the site. Complete the facility property damage checklist (*Appendix 12*). Take detailed notes on all damage and take photographs, if possible.
- Take detailed notes on all damaged assets. Record the item description, item number, and quantity. Be realistic when estimating quantities.
- Test all equipment before use. If equipment needs repair, contact company-approved vendors for the specific equipment.
- Keep accurate records for hours spent by employees and outside vendors for clean-up or emergency repairs.
- Keep receipts for any expenses incurred for emergency repairs or replacement or for expedient replenishment of equipment, inventory, etc.
- Keep accurate records as to when sites are closed, by day and number of business hours, including financial information on lost revenues and any continued expenses during the shutdown period.
- Coordinate with the appropriate company management representatives prior to reopening the impacted facility(ies). Note date and time that the site reopened, together with the site's normal business hours.
- Report any public or governmental order affecting site operation.
- Report on activity of other businesses in the vicinity or any unusual activity or extraordinary conditions occurring in the vicinity.
- Fill out the company incident report form (*Appendix 13*). Attach additional pages of documentation with the incident report if necessary.
- Send the completed incident report form along with all documentation to the appropriate company department.

Return to Normal Operations

The main objective of a BCP is to bring the company back to normal operations. If it is not possible to return to the precrisis normal, a new normal should be established. This new normal creates the expectation that, while there may be changes and restructuring in the workplace, the organization will phase back into productive work. Each step of the process and all decisions should be carefully documented.

As a rule, it is at this point that the crisis may be officially declared over. Again, it is important to document this decision. Press conferences and mass media communications may be undertaken to bolster employee and client confidence.

Corrective Action Plan

Any time a simulation exercise or an actual crises occurs a postmortem should be performed. If any failures, deficiencies, or weaknesses in the BCP are identified during the postmortem, a corrective action plan should be created. This documentation is then used to guide changes to the BCP in order to improve the process and avoid future problems.

When evaluating the response to an event, simulated or otherwise, notes should be gathered about what went well and what could be improved upon. This evaluation should include people, processes, and resources. It may be helpful to note that the NFPA 1600 Standard[8] categorizes corrective actions as follows:

1. Plan or standard operating procedures (SOP) revisions
2. Training
3. Equipment additions or modifications and facilities

Once the corrective action plan is completed, the results should be used to guide the necessary modifications to the existing BCP. As with any changes to the BCP, the BCP team should plan for and perform the appropriate training and exercise(s) to ensure the changes are communicated and prepared for.

How Do I Maintain a Business Continuity Program in the Long Term?

The security team should consistently emphasize throughout the organization that the business continuity program (BCP) is a living document that is continuously improved and adjusted; for instance, as lessons are learned through responses and exercises, or a change occurs in the risk environment, the BCP must be updated. In addition, the company's BCP advisory committee must conduct a formal periodic review of the BCP to confirm that it has been fully implemented and is meeting its objectives. A periodic evaluation is beneficial to program management, authorities, and other stakeholders because it confirms where the program is working correctly and where improvements are required. Information compiled from an evaluation can be used to assess program performance and aids in setting priorities for program improvements.

BCP SUPPORT AND ANNUAL STRATEGIC PLANNING

Another imperative for continuous review and evaluation relates to budgeting and company-wide planning. Organization budgets and strategic plans should incorporate funding and requirements for the BCP and will hopefully include the BCP as an annual strategic priority. To accommodate this, BCP review and evaluation must remain connected to other company planning cycles.

For example, many organizations review strategic priorities on an annual basis in preparation for the fiscal new year. During this review period, budget decisions are being made. Funding related to the BCP should be considered during this time. As management makes decisions about upcoming strategic goals, the BCP must be examined to ensure it is aligned with and incorporates any changes to the organization's business operations. To further illustrate this point, the following figure (derived from "The Emergency Management Planning Guide 2010–2011" issued by Public Safety Canada) illustrates an organization's proposed planning cycle. This cycle requires periodic and annual focus on BCP planning rather than the limited evaluation that occurs after an incident.

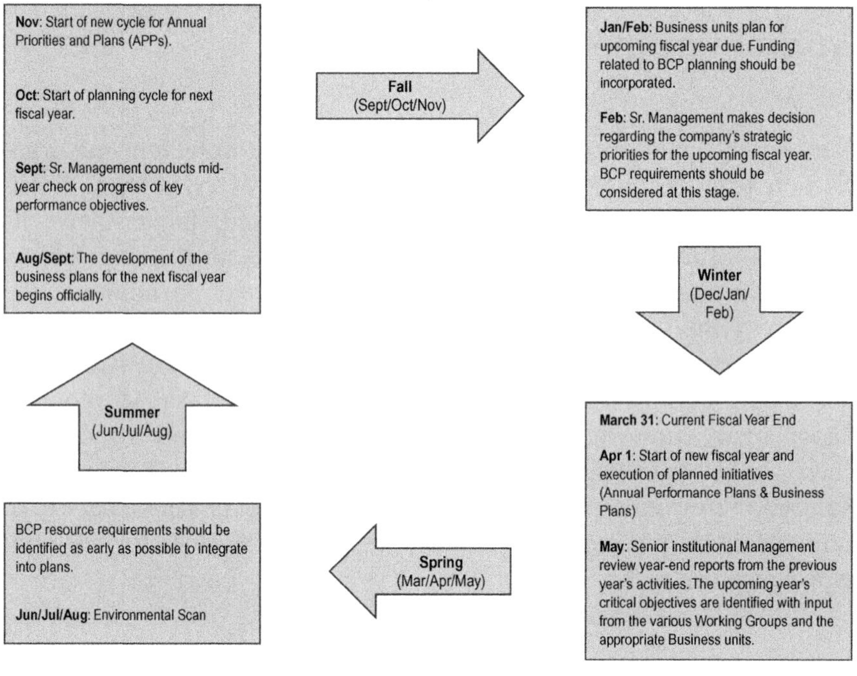

Example planning cycle (periodic and annual) for an organization's BCP.

APPENDIX 1

Specific Job Descriptions and Salary Ranges

Note: These job descriptions are reprinted with permission from Security Careers: Defining Jobs, Compensation, Qualifications, *2nd edition, by Steve Walker and Jerry Brennan, 2010: The Security Executive Council.*[9]

A. MANAGER, EMERGENCY PREPAREDNESS/ DISASTER RECOVERY

Job Description

This position is responsible for the business strategies associated with the emergency preparedness/disaster recovery function within the organization. The person who fills this position is accountable for overall planning, directing, and organizing activities of the programs, and ensuring their effective operation.

- Plans, develops, and manages the corporate emergency preparedness/ disaster recovery programs for the company under senior management direction.
- Implements policies, procedures, and systems required for maintaining and enhancing the overall emergency preparedness/disaster recovery mission.
- Oversees the architecture of recovery systems to include data systems, and data networks to ensure the integrity and security of all electronics data and data systems are adequately protected. This includes: procedure writing; program planning; project design and scheduling; development and delivering training; planning and conducting drills and exercises; designing, developing, and maintaining emergency response facilities and equipment.
- Designs, develops, and conducts drills and exercises.
- Plans, schedules and conducts a wide range of very complex facility and/or site emergency preparedness/disaster recovery drills which could include emergency response training drills, medical drills, fire response drills, nuclear incident monitoring drills, and protective action drills. Determines the need for emergency plans changes and

new procedures, and ensures the appropriate government format and content are followed.
- Coordinates with state and local emergency management authorities.
- Maintains expert knowledge of the organization's processes and hazards, interfaces with engineering and operations staff to ensure appropriate development of a facility and/or site-specific hazard assessment and emergency classification procedures.
- Prepares technical reports based on the expert interpretation of analyzed data.

Qualification Guidelines

Master's degree in studies relevant to this position and more than six years of emergency management/disaster recovery experience with a major corporation and/or law enforcement, intelligence, public service or private sector security organization; or a bachelor's degree in studies relevant to this position and more than 10 years emergency management/disaster recovery experience.

B. SENIOR EMERGENCY PREPAREDNESS SPECIALIST IV

Job Description

- Works under consultative direction toward predetermined goals and objectives.
- Assignments are usually self-initiated. Determines and pursues courses of action necessary to obtain desired results.
- Exercises technical discretion within broadly defined practices and policies in selecting methods, techniques and evaluation criterion for obtaining results.
- Oversees the design, development and maintenance of the organization's emergency preparedness program. This could include: procedure writing; program planning; project design and scheduling; development and delivering training; planning and conducting drills and exercises; designing, developing and maintaining emergency response facilities and equipment.
- Designs, develops, and conducts drills and exercises.
- May manage the scenario development portion of schedule.
- May act as the senior team leader to plan, schedule and conduct a wide range of very complex facility and/or site emergency preparedness drills which could include emergency response training drills,

medical drills, fire response drills, nuclear incident monitoring drills, and protective action drills.

- Determines the need for emergency plans changes and new procedures, and ensures the appropriate government format and content are followed.
- May coordinate with state and local emergency management authorities.
- With expert knowledge of the organization's processes and hazards, interfaces with engineering and operations staff to ensure appropriate development of a facility and/or site-specific hazard assessment and emergency classification procedures.
- Prepares technical reports based on the expert interpretation of analyzed data.
- Provides leadership to less experienced specialist and to technicians through work assignments, monitoring schedules and resolving problems.
- May act as lead person or technical expert on projects.

Qualification Guidelines

Bachelor's degree in an area of study relevant to this position and more than eight years of experience in emergency management with law enforcement, or public or private sector security organization.

C. EMERGENCY PREPAREDNESS SPECIALIST III

Job Description

- Works under very general direction.
- Exercises reasonable latitude in determining technical objectives of assignments. Work is reviewed upon completion for adequacy in meeting objectives.
- Works on problems of diverse scope and complexity where analysis of data requires evaluation of identifiable factors.
- Uses technical discretion within generally defined practices and policies in selecting methods and techniques for obtaining solutions.
- Participates in designing, developing and maintaining the organization's emergency preparedness program. This could include: procedure writing; program planning; project design and scheduling; development and delivering training; planning and conducting drills and exercises; designing, developing and maintaining emergency response facilities and equipment.

- Conducts emergency preparedness drills and exercises. May oversee the scenario development portion of schedule.
- Assists in design and development of training lesson plans and conducts procedure training.
- May lead a project team to plan, schedule and conduct a wide range of complex facility and/or site emergency preparedness drills, which could include emergency response training drills, medical drills, fire response drills, nuclear incident monitoring drills, and protective action drills.
- Participates in identifying the need for emergency plan changes and new procedures, and ensures the appropriate government format and content are followed.
- Provides coordination with state and local emergency management authorities.
- With good working knowledge of the organization's processes and hazards, interfaces with engineering and operations staff to ensure appropriate development of a facility and/or site-specific hazard assessment and emergency classification procedures.
- May provide leadership to less experienced specialist and to technicians through work assignments, monitoring schedules and resolving problems. May also act as lead person or technical expert on small to medium projects.

Qualification Guidelines

Bachelor's degree in an area of study relevant to this position and more than six years of experience in emergency management with a law enforcement, public or private sector security organization. Certification preferred.

APPENDIX 2

Advisory Committee Members

Name	Function	Phone Number	Email Address

APPENDIX 3

Corporate Contingency Planning Umbrella

On the next page you will find a full version of the corporate contingency planning umbrella.

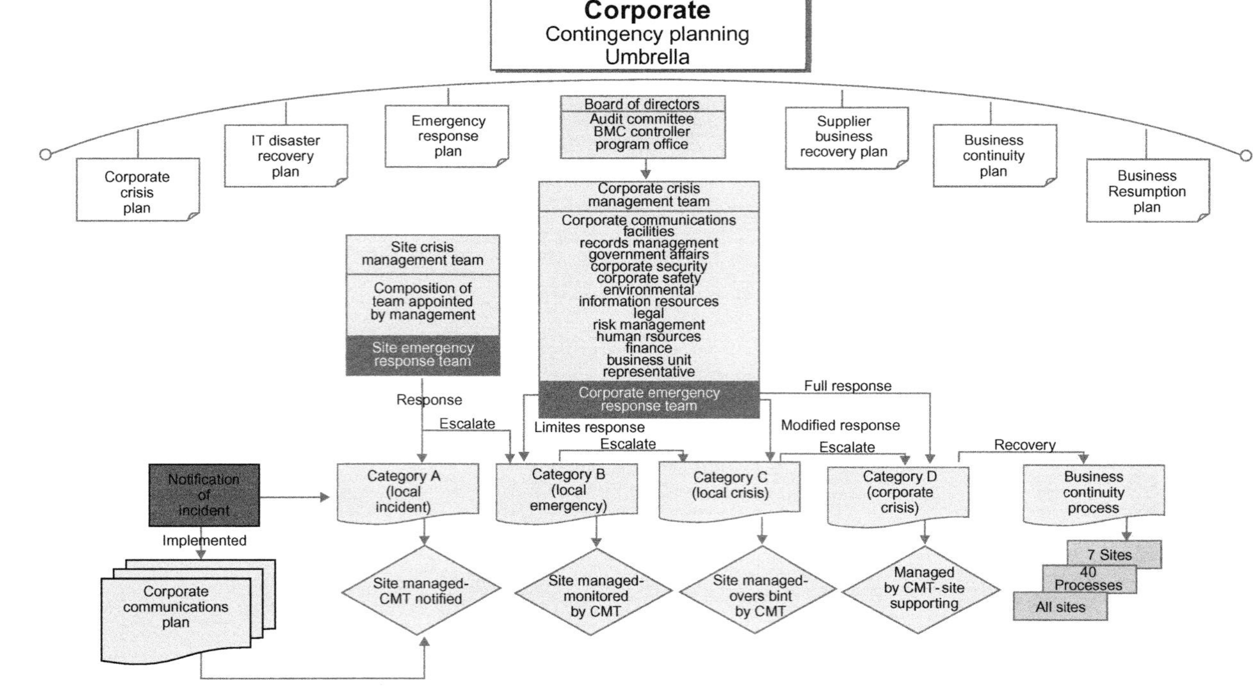

Corporate
Contingency planning
Umbrella
Corporate crisis plan
IT disaster recovery plan
Emergency response plan
Board of directors
Audit committee
BMC controller
program office
Supplier business recovery plan
Business continuity plan
Business Resumption plan
Corporate crisis management team
Corporate communications
facilities
records management
government affairs
corporate security
corporate safety
environmental
information resources
legal
risk management
human rsources
finance
business unit
representative
Corporate emergency response team
Site crisis management team
Composition of team appointed by management
Site emergency response team
Response
Escalate
Limites response
Escalate
Full response
Modified response
Escalate
Recovery
Notification of incident
Implemented
Corporate communications plan
Category A (local incident)
Category B (local emergency)
Category C (local crisis)
Category D (corporate crisis)
Business continuity process
Site managed-CMT notified
Site managed-monitored by CMT
Site managed-overs bint by CMT
Managed by CMT-site supporting
7 Sites
40 Processes
All sites
Process development - role definition – approvals – rollout – monitor – valldata – train – exerolse – inoident analysis – debriefing – after action – lessons learned

APPENDIX 4

Threat Risk Matrix and Heat Map

The matrix below is an example of how threats can be reviewed in order to determine their severity and is based on recommendations found in the ASIS Business Continuity Guideline. The threats included here are not meant to be all-encompassing and should be customized according to the organization's specific needs and risks.

RATINGS LEGEND

Rate "Impact" as: 1 = Negligible; 2 = Some; 3 = Moderate; 4 = Significant; 5 = Severe

Rate "Probability" as: 1 = Very Low; 2 = Low; 3 = Medium; 4 = High; 5 = Very High

Probability × Impact = Risk Rating

Threat	Impact	Probability	Risk Rating
Bombing			
Workplace violence			
Robbery			
Supply chain disruption			
Loss of key talent			
Loss of key supplier			
Hurricane			
Fire			
Pandemic			
Tsunami			
Product contamination			
Information systems disruption			
Loss of proprietary information			
Foreign exchange fluctuation			
Power failure			
Work stoppage			

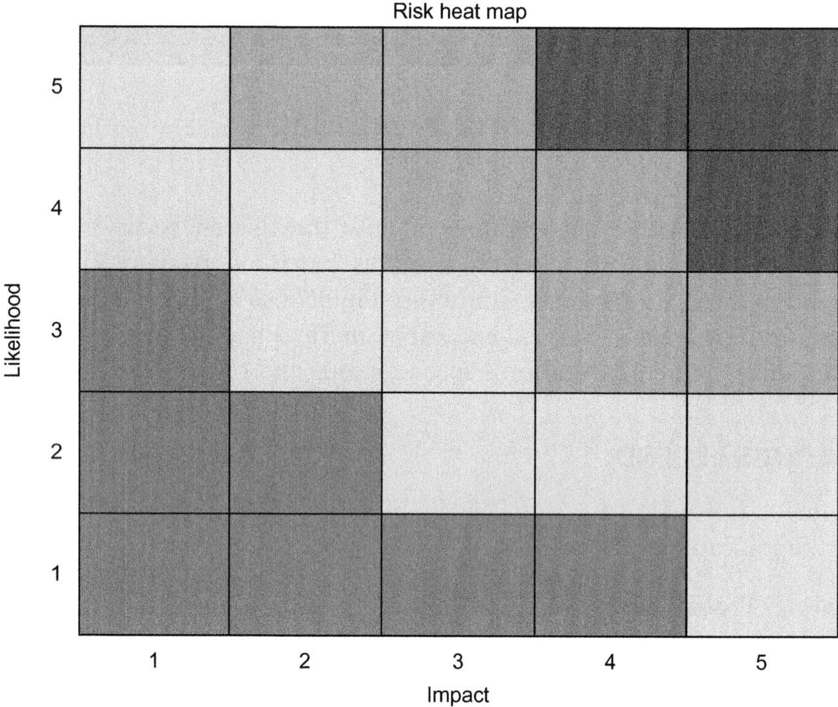

For this example, 1 = low, 5 = high

The color of the cells shown above is only an example.
The actual determination which cells have which colors is up to the user of the chart.

When assessing risk level, values always go to the lower number when in doubt.

APPENDIX 5

Business Impact Analysis Template

Included in this appendix is an example business impact analysis (BIA) template that is available from the Centers for Disease Control and Prevention: http://www2.cdc.gov/cdcup/library/templates/default.htm#.UTYbiKugYfw. It contains the necessary elements common to most BIA forms and can be used to elicit responses for use in an effective BCP risk assessment. The collection of this data is helpful for identifying the most critical business functions and the impact of a disruption to those operations may cause.

<PROJECT NAME>

BUSINESS IMPACT ANALYSIS

Version *<1.0>*

<mm/dd/yyyy>

[Insert appropriate disclaimer(s)]

VERSION HISTORY

[Provide information on how the development and distribution of the Business Impact Analysis was controlled and tracked. Use the table below to provide the version number, the author implementing the version, the date of the version, the name of the person approving the version, the date that particular version was approved, and a brief description of the reason for creating the revised version.]

Version #	Implemented By	Revision Date	Approved By	Approval Date	Reason
1.0	*<Author name>*	*<mm/dd/yy>*	*<name>*	*<mm/dd/yy>*	*<reason>*

UP Template Version: 06/30/08

Note to the Author

[This document is a template of a ***Business Impact Analysis*** *document for a project. The template includes instructions to the author, boilerplate text, and fields that should be replaced with the values specific to the project.*

- *Blue italicized text enclosed in square brackets ([text]) provides instructions to the document author, or describes the intent, assumptions and context for content included in this document.*
- *Blue italicized text enclosed in angle brackets (<text>) indicates a field that should be replaced with information specific to a particular project.*
- *Text and tables in black are provided as boilerplate examples of wording and formats that may be used or modified as appropriate to a specific project. These are offered only as suggestions to assist in developing project documents; they are not mandatory formats.*

When using this template for your project document, it is recommended that you follow these steps:

1. *Replace all text enclosed in angle brackets (e.g.,, <Project Name>) with the correct field values. These angle brackets appear in both the body of the document and in headers and footers. To customize fields in Microsoft Word (which display a gray background when selected):*
    a. *Select File>Properties>Summary and fill in the Title field with the Document Name and the Subject field with the Project Name.*
    b. *Select File>Properties>Custom and fill in the Last Modified, Status, and Version fields with the appropriate information for this document.*
    c. *After you click OK to close the dialog box, update the fields throughout the document with these values by selecting Edit>Select All (or Ctrl-A) and pressing F9. Or you can update an individual field by clicking on it and pressing F9. This must be done separately for Headers and Footers.*
2. *Modify boilerplate text as appropriate to the specific project.*
3. *To add any new sections to the document, ensure that the appropriate header and body text styles are maintained. Styles used for the Section Headings are Heading 1, Heading 2 and Heading 3. Style used for boilerplate text is Body Text.*
4. *To update the Table of Contents, right-click and select "Update field" and choose the option- "Update entire table"*
5. *Before submission of the first draft of this document, delete this "Notes to the Author" page and all instructions to the author, which appear throughout the document as blue italicized text enclosed in square brackets.]*

TABLE OF CONTENTS

1 INTRODUCTION **5**
1.1 Purpose 5
2 SYSTEM INFORMATION **5**
2.1 Points of Contact 5
2.2 System Resources 5
2.3 Critical Contacts and Resources 6
2.4 Disruption Impact 6
2.5 Resource Recovery Priority 6
APPENDIX A: BUSINESS IMPACT ANALYSIS APPROVAL **7**
APPENDIX B: REFERENCES **8**
APPENDIX C: KEY TERMS **9**

1 INTRODUCTION

1.1 PURPOSE

The Business Impact Analysis (BIA) is an essential step in the development of a contingency/disaster recovery plan.
[Enter purpose of this specific BIA]

2 SYSTEM INFORMATION

Date: *<Enter date BIA completed>*
Point of Contact (POC): *<Enter BIA POC>*

Organization: *<Enter Organization>*
System Name: *<Enter name>*
System Manager: *<Enter manager>*
System Description: *<Enter description>*

2.1 POINTS OF CONTACT

[Enter the name and description of individuals, positions, offices, etc of points-of-contact related to the content contained within this BIA.]

Internal Contacts

- ***<Enter Name>***: *<Enter description of role as it relates to this BIA>*
- ***<Enter Name>***: *<Enter description of role as it relates to this BIA>*
- ***<Enter Name>***: *<Enter description of role as it relates to this BIA>*

External Contacts

[Enter the name and description of individuals, positions, offices, etc of points-of-contact related to the content contained within this BIA.]

- ***<Enter Name>***: *<Enter description of role as it relates to this BIA>*
- ***<Enter Name>***: *<Enter description of role as it relates to this BIA>*
- ***<Enter Name>***: *<Enter description of role as it relates to this BIA>*

2.2 SYSTEM RESOURCES

[Enter the category, name, and description of resources related to, referenced, and/or analyzed within as part of this BIA.]

Hardware

- ***<Enter Name>***: *<Enter description of resource>*
- ***<Enter Name>***: *<Enter description of resource>*
- ***<Enter Name>***: *<Enter description of resource>*

Software

- ***<Enter Name>***: *<Enter description of resource>*
- ***<Enter Name>***: *<Enter description of resource>*
- ***<Enter Name>***: *<Enter description of resource>*

Other

- ***<Enter Name>***: *<Enter description of resource>*
- ***<Enter Name>***: *<Enter description of resource>*
- ***<Enter Name>***: *<Enter description of resource>*

2.3 CRITICAL CONTACTS AND RESOURCES

[Relate critical contacts, their roles, and critical resources from the content entered into the previous two sections and relate them to each other.]

Critical Contacts/Roles	Critical Resources
<Enter Name>	• *<Enter critical resource name>* • *<Enter critical resource name>* • *<Enter critical resource name>*
	•

2.4 DISRUPTION IMPACT

[Identify disruption impacts and allowable outage times. Characterize the impact on critical roles if a critical resource is unavailable. Identify the maximum acceptable period that the resource could be unavailable before unacceptable impacts resulted.]

Resource	Outage Impact	Allowable Outage
<Enter Resource Name>	*<Enter description of outage impact>*	*<Enter description of allowable outage time>*

2.5 RESOURCE RECOVERY PRIORITY

[List the order of recovery priority for all resources Identified earlier in this document. Identify and describe an appropriate priority scale such as high, medium, low; 1, 2, 3; etc.]

Priority	Resource	Comments
<priority>	*<Enter Resource Name>*	*<Enter additional comments >*

Appendix A: Business Impact Analysis Approval

The undersigned acknowledge they have reviewed the *<Project Name>* **Business Impact Analysis** and agree with the approach it presents. Changes to this **Business Impact Analysis** will be coordinated with and approved by the undersigned or their designated representatives.

[List the individuals whose signatures are desired. Examples of such individuals are Business Steward, Implementation Manager or Project Sponsor. Add additional lines for signature as necessary. Although signatures are desired, they are not always required to move forward with the practices outlined within this document.]

Signature: ______________________________ Date: ____________

Print Name: ______________________________

Title: ______________________________

Role: ______________________________

Signature: ______________________________ Date: ____________

Print Name: ______________________________

Title: ______________________________

Role: ______________________________

Signature: ______________________________ Date: ____________

Print Name: ______________________________

Title: ______________________________

Role: ______________________________

APPENDIX B: REFERENCES

[Insert the name, version number, description, and physical location of any documents referenced in this document. Add rows to the table as necessary.]

The following table summarizes the documents referenced in this document.

Document Name and Version	Description	Location
<Document Name and Version Number>	*[Provide description of the document]*	*<URL or Network path where document is located>*

APPENDIX C: KEY TERMS

[Insert terms and definitions used in this document. Add rows to the table as necessary. Follow the link below to for definitions of project management terms and acronyms used in this and other documents.

http://www2.cdc.gov/cdcup/library/other/help.htm

The following table provides definitions for terms relevant to this document.

Term	Definition
[Insert Term]	*[Provide definition of the term used in this document.]*
[Insert Term]	*[Provide definition of the term used in this document.]*
[Insert Term]	*[Provide definition of the term used in this document.]*

APPENDIX 6

CMT/IMT/LRT Member List

Primary Member	Function	Cell Phone	Home Phone	Backup Member	Function	Cell Phone	Home Phone
*Designate CMT, IMT, and LRT leads with an *.*							

APPENDIX 7

CMT, IMT, and LRT Member Roles and Responsibilities

CMT LEAD

- Organizes and calls meetings.
- Determines which active members and subject-matter experts (SMEs) will participate in the CMT meetings.
- Aligns CMT on roles and responsibilities at the first meeting.
- Keeps minutes and tracks commitments.
- Drives for team alignment on action steps when immediate incident response is required.
- Works in collaboration with IMT lead to determine when it is appropriate to notify or convene the CMT.
- Helps company determine other internal/external stakeholders to represent business units as decision makers.
- Organizes future meetings.
- Creates and distributes communications to correct audiences.

IMT LEAD

- Evaluates incident level.
- Organizes and calls meetings.
- Determines which active members and SMEs will participate in the IMT meetings.
- Aligns IMT on roles and responsibilities at the first meeting.
- Keeps minutes and tracks commitments.
- Drives for team alignment on action steps when immediate incident response is required.
- Works in collaboration with LRT lead (if necessary) to determine appropriate incident communication to the CMT lead.
- Helps company determine other internal/external stakeholders to represent business units as decision makers.

- Organizes future meetings.
- Creates and distributes communications to correct audiences.

LRT LEAD

The LRT lead is responsible for presiding over all local response efforts. He or she is the final decision authority in all elements of the response and serves as a liaison with the IMT when additional support, resources, or guidance is needed.

- Convenes the LRT.
- Utilizes the critical incident goals and guiding principles to set direction.
- Approves market-level decisions as they relate to the incident.
- Discusses with IMT lead the benefits of sending additional employees to support the LRT.
- Works with global communications to establish a communications strategy.
- Ensures alignment on organizational designee to speak to the media.

CMT, IMT, AND LRT MEMBER

- Participates in requested crisis management meetings.
- May join other meetings as an optional attendee.
- Helps company determine other internal/external stakeholders to represent business units as decision makers.
- Participates in the identification of SME needs.
- Identifies potential escalation of circumstances.
- Provides communications of incident within their function.

SUBJECT-MATTER EXPERT

- Contributes expert opinion.
- Offers strategic options.
- Highlights negative ramifications prior to plan implementation.
- Assists CMT and/or IMT as required to determine the correct decision makers in ongoing incident.

SPECIFIC IMT MEMBER ROLES AND RESPONSIBILITIES

Depending on the size of a company's organization and scope of the incident, the individual member roles and responsibilities outlined below may become blended with other functions.

HUMAN RESOURCES

- Coordinate needs with the human resources LRT member including securing necessary employee assistance program (EAP) services.
- Clarify and communicate with the human resources LRT member his/her expected roles and responsibilities prior to arrival.
- Travel to the incident location to support if required.
- Coordinate senior executive visits if required.
- If the incident involves a serious injury or death:
  - Between 12 and 48 hours after a serious injury or death, a member of the senior leadership team should visit the families of employee(s) with serious or fatal injuries.
  - Before the visit, background information will be prepared by corporate communications lead to greet the family appropriately. Assist with the collection of the names and pertinent information about family members, their requests and needs, and personal information about the employee(s). Corporate communications will also provide a statement from the partner's manager and any messages of encouragement/condolence from partners.
- The senior leader should consider bringing up to two others on the visit. Consider a mental health specialist and a human resources manager.
- The senior leader(s) should attend funerals or memorials as appropriate and be prepared to speak at these if asked by the family.
- Support human resources employees in communications and arrangement of counseling services.
- Identify at-risk individuals.
- Contact the company's benefits department to begin creating a strategy for addressing the emotional needs of employees who are affected by the crisis.
- Obtain a list of counselor names that would be able to provide services in the affected areas.

- Consider bringing counselors from other areas since there will be a limited number of counselors available in the affected areas.
- Create and communicate a schedule for counselors to be available for one-on-one and group sessions with employees in a convenient but private location.
- Consider the need of follow-up training for managers and leadership team members in the affected area, focusing on how to recognize and support employees experiencing event related trauma.
- Discuss back-to-work transitions.
- Offer outreach, volunteer and giving programs.

SECURITY

- Confirm the facts of the incident reported with law enforcement officials.
- Clarify and communicate with their LRT representative the expected roles and responsibilities prior to arrival. Determine whether it will be necessary to lead security efforts or perform as a supporting function for local teams.
- Travel to the incident location if necessary.
- Act as liaison with law enforcement for investigation updates and status (assist with evidence gathering and retrieval).
  - Secure the crime scene after release by law enforcement.
  - Conduct a company investigation.
  - Canvas neighboring businesses for additional evidence.
  - Interview partners and witnesses. Coordinate with human resources where the implications of the actions of an employee require disciplinary action.
  - Support investigative walk through with insurance company.
  - Support securing damaged locations.
  - Support employee or family member protection/assistance.
  - Coordinate outside security services for postevent activities as needed.
  - Support impacted employee family members as appropriate.

INTERNAL AND EXTERNAL COMMUNICATIONS

- Confirm the facts of the incidents.
- Clarify and communicate with their LRT representative the expected roles and responsibilities prior to arrival. Determine if it is

necessary to lead media efforts or perform a supporting function for local teams.
- Travel to the incident location if needed.
- Determine appropriate company and/or regional spokespeople and who will communicate to media and lead employee communications.
- Write and distribute briefing documents for senior leadership (i.e., media statements, employee and family background information) as an element of overall communication strategy.
- Accompany and provide support to spokespeople traveling to site.
- Be the strategic internal and external communications lead on the official company position and messaging by preparing media statements, key messages, talking points, Q&A, and employee communications such as voicemail and email.
- Provide strategic communications to field teams when they draft of media statements, key messages, talking points, and Q&A.
- Prepare and gain approval of all communication documents.
- Log and respond to all media inquiries.
- Log and facilitate response to phone communications and inquiries.
- Arrange for the company and local media statement to be sent via wire or taped feed.
- Coordinate with local public relations firm to arrange for a local press conference or live feed of taped statement from local spokesperson (specific steps will be different in each market).
- Report daily on media coverage and employee and customer enquiries.

BUSINESS CONTINUITY

- Confirm the facts of the incident reported with operations employees on site.
- Clarify and communicate with their LRT representative the expected roles and responsibilities prior to arrival. Determine whether it will be necessary to lead operational efforts or perform a supporting function for local teams.
- Discuss and clarify ongoing business continuity requirements with on-site leadership team.
- Travel to the incident location.

- Work with the IMT in order to act as liaison between the site and the CMT in order to coordinate company resources. These may include:
  - Focus on potential mitigation/risk control and business continuity steps.
  - Support CMT, IMT, and LRT efforts as necessary (EAP meetings, partner communication, senior management visits, etc.).
  - Consolidate travel plans for all traveling employees from the company's global office for reference.
  - Discuss with each individual traveling employee what their needs will be.
  - Coordinate supplies as appropriate.
  - Personally confirm all traveling employees' roles before arriving at incident site.
  - Hold a traveling employee group meeting at the company's global office before leaving, at airport or offsite near the incident. Confirm roles, responsibilities, communications methods and expectations, incident-specific details, check-in procedures, and future travel plans.
  - Coordinate/facilitate ongoing communications between the home office and site teams.
  - Maintain working documentation of events and actions.
  - Link with communications team for any necessary market/region/division messaging.
  - Handle any other needs for the field with other support departments as required.
  - Ensure that the company's global departments are aware of any changes to normal operational procedures.
  - Facilitate additional requirements with global departments as required for the event.
  - Coordinate additional on-site resources needed (meeting locations, accommodation, etc.).
  - Coordinate operational support for local authorities (water, coffee, donations, communication, etc.).

SPECIFIC LRT MEMBER ROLES AND RESPONSIBILITIES

The following information should serve as a guide to build a regional LRT.

Operations Representative (as Designated)

The operations representative is responsible for managing the implementation of all tactical preparation, response, and recovery elements. They serve as the liaison between site employees and the LRT.

- Report on the incident's effect on employees (location, safety, and needs).
- Report on the incident's effect on employees' attendance (closures, openings, and adjustments).
- Provide an operational prospective on all elements of response plan.
- Manage the execution of the response plan with appropriate teams.
- Ensure open and direct communication during the response and recovery phases.

Human Resources Representative

The human resources representative is responsible to provide a human resource perspective and counsel in all areas of preparation, response, and recovery. He or she serves as an advocate for all employees and ensures the appropriate support resources are available to all employees.

- Provide a human resource perspective on all elements of the response plan. Assist employees in accessing company resource services.
- Coordinate on-site EAP visits as necessary.

Marketing Representative

The marketing representative is responsible for managing all proactive and reactive statements under the direction of global communications. He or she serves as the liaison between local governmental agencies, nonprofit organizations, and the LRT.

- Provide a marketing perspective on all elements of the response plan.
- Coordinate with local public relations to address local media requests for information or prescripted reactionary statements.

Facilities Representative

The facilities representative is responsible for implementing preparation and recovery steps for all facilities.

- Provide facilities perspective on all elements of the response plan.
- Coordinate vendor availability to secure facilities.
- Coordinate damage assessment visits to impacted facilities.
- Record and report on damage from field assessments.
- Coordinate repairs and cleanup of facilities with vendors or internal company departments.

Security Representative

The security representative is responsible for ensuring that the safety and security of sites and employees remain a priority during the adjustments in activities that may occur during an event. He or she serves as the liaison between local government authorities and the LRT.

- Provide people and asset protection perspective on all elements of the response plan.
- Confirm the facts of the incident reported with law enforcement officials as applicable.
- Coordinate with alarm monitoring companies to ensure responses are directed accordingly.
- Coordinate security-related needs for partners and facilities as applicable.

Supply Chain Representative

The supply chain representative is responsible for ensuring appropriate and timely adjustments to all site deliveries. He or she serves as the liaison between local vendors and the LRT.

- Provide supply chain perspective on all elements of the response plan.
- Anticipate impact to deliveries and distribution.
- Coordinate alternate delivery times or delay to deliveries based on the impacts of the critical incident.
- Recommend adjustments to distributed products.
- Record and report on potential impacts to distribution.

Information Systems Representative

The information systems representative serves as the liaison between local vendors and the LRT.

- Provide information systems perspective on all elements of the response plan.

- Anticipate, record, and report impact to the company's information systems.
- Coordinate short- and long-term recovery solutions based on the impacts of the critical incident on the company's information systems.

APPENDIX 8

Crisis Management Meeting Locations and Contacts

The company's primary and secondary meeting locations are located at:

- Primary meeting location—insert full address and phone number
- Secondary meeting location—insert full address and phone number

In the table below, insert critical company phone numbers needed to manage an incident. These may include:

- Conference call lines and PINs
- Facility, office, and meeting location numbers
- EOC phone number
- Company hotline numbers—media, benefits, etc.

Name/Contact	Telephone	Cell Phone
Site manager		
Assistant site manager		
Regional manager		
Company security contact		
Primary meeting location: ____________		
Secondary meeting location: __________		
Regional office		
Contracted security company		
Building/site management		
Local police	911	911
Local hospital: ______________		
Bus/train info line		
Taxi		
Neighboring site: ____________		
Neighboring site: ____________		
Incident reporting hotline		—
Conference call line and PIN		—
Emergency operations center (EOC)		—
Vendor: ____________________		
Vendor: ____________________		

APPENDIX 9

CMT/IMT Meeting Agenda

MEETING GROUND RULES

- Participants are restricted to CMT/IMT primary members unless requested by the IMT lead.
- If a CMT/IMT primary member is unavailable, the designated back-up should attend in their place.
- Each CMT/IMT primary member should assemble his or her functional team at a location as close to the meeting location as possible, in order to receive updates or action plans.
- The CMT/IMT lead will facilitate the meeting and is responsible for leading the team through the IMT meeting agenda.
- The elements identified in part I of the agenda are intended to guide the CMT/IMT members through the response portion of an incident. There may be times when members may focus on these elements until the incident is stabilized.
- Once stability is achieved, part II elements should be addressed to further support containment.

MEETING AGENDA PART I

- CMT/IMT leads update CMT/IMT Members on the situation and review the site situation checklist (SSC).
- Outline the relevant pieces from each CMT/IMT member's perspective addressing the response plan topics in the following order:
  - Life safety
  - Business implications
  - Communications strategy
- Assess the impact to business units, departments, and operations.
- Determine if the incident has the potential for external focus.
- Use the critical incident decision matrix to prioritize major decisions into A, B, and C decisions (see below).

- Determine what additional information needs to be secured to make a priority decision.
  - Is there time to gather more information or do time constraints demand immediate next steps?
- Identify additional sources or information necessary to support decision making.
- Focus around three key areas when making a decision:
  1. What actions need to stop?
  2. What actions need to start?
  3. How can the situation escalate in severity?
     - Can this escalation be prevented?
- Confirm the initial communications plan(s) including strategy, message, and method, and identify an appropriate spokesperson.
- Determine if members of senior management or other stakeholders should travel to the incident site.
  - If yes, assign a member of the IMT to coordinate the schedule, travel, and communication arrangements.
- Make recommendation(s) on additional participants for follow-up meetings.
- Approve communications statement(s). Included in this is an update to the CMT/IMT.
- Identify other employees, customers, vendors, and investors that may need to receive communications regarding the incident.
- Monitor media attention and ensure web site(s), marketing message(s), and call centers are conveying appropriate messages.
- Confirm next meetings including time, location, and participants.

MEETING AGENDA PART II

- CMT/IMT leads update CMT/IMT Members on the situation and review the site situation checklist.
- Receive a situational update from each CMT/IMT Member.
- Determine the appropriate representative to communicate with family members of affected employees as necessary.
- Approve the identified spokesperson to address the media and set press conference schedule.
- Confirm call centers are redirecting critical incident calls to the correct location.
- Determine action steps and timeline for recovery activities.
- Adjust communications strategy based on new recovery schedule.

LRT MEETING AGENDA

It is recommended that the LRT review each of the agenda items during their meetings or conference calls to ensure alignment of discussion and tangible and tactical items are covered. Each incident is different and has different impacts and not all topics may be covered.

OPERATIONS

Situational Update

- What is the situation and what information is confirmed and unconfirmed?
- Are employees, customers, facilities, or the community directly impacted?
- Have facilities, or will facilities be, closed?
- What operational decisions have already been made and communicated out?
- What are the responses from neighboring business'?

Life Safety

- What is the plan to account for all impacted employees, customers, and vendors?
- Have there been any employee, customer, or vendor injuries?
- What is the plan to mitigate future risks to employee, customers, and vendors?

HUMAN RESOURCES

- What steps need to be taken for payroll processing and check delivery?
- Have affected employees received information on available resources?
- Is EAP required for individuals or at a group/store level?
- How will missed shifts be handled?
- What is the pay policy for this incident (Inclement weather policy? Catastrophic policy? Other?)?

SECURITY

- What are the reports from local authorities?
- Are conditions safe for employees, customers, and vendors?

- What is the level of security for the facility(ies)?
- What additional measures need to be put in place to increase security?

SUPPLY CHAIN

- What adjustments need to be made to orders and deliveries?

FACILITIES

- What steps have been taken to secure facilities?
- When will damage assessments occur?
- What is the repair schedule and process?

MEDIA/MARKETING

- Is there a need for media statements?
- Has information in media statements been verified accordingly?
- Are there any marketing programs that may need to be rescheduled/ cancelled due to the incident?
- How are stores providing support to the local responders and the community?
- Is there a need for corporate donations to response organizations?

COMMUNICATIONS

- What has been communicated internally and externally thus far?
- What media sources are being used to collect information (i.e., television, web sites, word of mouth, local authorities, etc.)?
- What is the communication strategy?
  - Who will be communicating?
  - What messaging needs to be sent?
- What are the audiences for the messaging (i.e., regional, divisional, company-wide, public, etc.)?
  - When do the messages need to be sent?
  - What communications vehicles will be used to deliver the messages?
  - What is the timeline for implementation?

APPENDIX 10

Critical Incident Decision Matrix

This matrix serves as a visual resource to assist in outlining and prioritizing group decisions that the IMT and LRT will need to make. It may serve as either a flip chart or a pin-up to communicate visual information during the meeting. When plotting the "Communication" action, be sure to include:

- The specific message(s)
- How and when the message(s) will be sent
- The audience(s) that will be receiving the message(s).

Priority	Life Safety	Business Issue	Communication
A Priorities (Immediate)			
B Priorities (Urgent)			
C Priorities (Limited)			
People/Group Responsible			
Completed Tasks			

APPENDIX 11

Critical Incident Individual Decision Matrix

This matrix provides IMT and LRT members with a method to prioritize group decisions for their specific business unit during the entire timeframe required to manage the crisis.

Priority Levels: A—Immediate; B—Urgent; C—Limited

Topic/ Action Item	Priority Level	Situation Specifics		Communication Strategy	Responsible Team Member	Completion Date/Time
		Life Safety	Business Implications			

APPENDIX 12

Facility Property Assessment Checklist

After the site has been cleared for reentry by local authorities or building management, authorized company personnel should use this tool to detail any damages.

Site #: __________

Completed By: _________________________

Date: __________

Site Exterior	Observed Physical Condition
Sidewalks	
Exterior signage (front, rear, and sides)	
Exterior walls of site (front and rear)	
Exterior glass windows	
Condition of building (front and rear)	
Driveways/parking lot	
View of roof/underneath canopy	
Exterior door(s)	
Are there other nearby building/center tenants open?	
Are there any other unusual occurrences in the area?	
Is there any order from a governmental agency?	
Did you speak with the on-site property manager/property owner?	

Site Interior	Observed Physical Condition
Interior Walls	
Floor/Floor Coverings	
Ceiling/Ceiling Tiles	
Interior Door(s)	
Displays	
Furniture/Tables and Chairs/Desks	
Interior Glass Windows	
Lighting	
Counters/Cabinets	
Other Physical Conditions Observed	
Are Utilities On or Off?	
Bathrooms	
Rear Door/Exit	
Entrance Doors (if applicable)	
Floor Coverings	
Wall Coverings	
Ceiling Tiles	
Shelving/Displays/Furniture/Desk	
Are Utilities On or Off?	

When completing the assessment, also be sure to document overall comments or unusual conditions that may inhibit the ability to operate this location.

APPENDIX 13

Incident Report

FOR INTERNAL USE ONLY

INCIDENT REPORT FORM

Report Incidents Within 24 Hours To ____________

For Customer/Employee Injury, Crime/Security Incidents and Company Property Damage

Complete this form with as much detail as possible. ***Please Print.***

Time & Place	Date of Incident________________ Time of Incident______________(AM/PM) Facility/Department Name/Number________________ State/Province__________ Facility/Department Phone Number (______)______________ Who assisted Customer/Employee? Facility/Department Manager________________ ______________ Video Evidence Available? ❑ Yes ❑ No ______________
Type Of Incident	**Mark appropriate box:** ❑ Customer Injury ❑ Damage to Customer Property / Property of Others ❑ Employee Injury ❑ Company Property ❑ Auto Damage ❑ Crime or Security-Related Incident
Employee or Customer Involved/ Injured	Name________________ Employee Number______________ Address________________ Best Number for Contact H or W (circle) City____________ St/Pr_____ Zip/PC________ Phone Number (____)____________(H) (____)____________(W)
Description Of Incident/ Injury **Statements Attached?** ❑ Y ❑ N	**LOCATION:** ❑ **In Facility** ❑ **Bathroom** ❑ **Sidewalk** ❑ **Parking Lot** ❑ **Car** ❑ **Other**________ Describe Incident in your own words. ______________________________ ______________________________ ______________________________ ______________________________ ______________________________ ______________________________ If Product/Equipment Involved: What is Product/Equipment?________________ ❑ Product/Equipment retrieved ? Or Other?______________ ❑ Ambulance/Fire Dept. Called ❑ First Aid: What was Administered?______________ ❑ Police Called Who Administered First Aid?______________ **Is Employee / Customer seeking professional medical attention?** ❑ **Y** ❑ **N**
Witnesses	Name______________ Phone Number (____)____________ Employee ❑ Y ❑ N Name______________ Phone Number (____)____________ Employee ❑ Y ❑ N Name______________ Phone Number (____)____________ Employee ❑ Y ❑ N
Follow Up	➢ **IMPORTANT: Report Incidents within 24 hours to** ____________ ➢ Keep and file this report in your office Incident Report file. **Reported by (SIGNATURE)** ________________ **Title**______________ **Print Name:**________________ **Date**______________

APPENDIX 14

Government Contacts

National emergency management agencies, such as FEMA in the USA, can be used to assist critical incident response in your area. Fill in local phone numbers in the spaces provided. Depending on the nature of the critical incident, different agencies may be in charge of the recovery effort. When trying to coordinate any details, start with your city's emergency management operations center (or equivalent) and then the state/province emergency management operations center; however, a recovery effort that will take a prolonged time will usually be handed over to your national emergency management agency.

Name of Organization	Contact Name	Phone Number
City emergency management operations center		
State/province emergency management operations center		
Regional emergency management operations center		
Police		
Fire department		
Mayor's office		
Department of health		
Building inspector		

REFERENCES

1. Livingston, G. (2011). *The Definitive Guide to Business Continuity Planning*. MIR3, Inc. Available from <http://www.mir3.com/get-the-definitive-guide-to-business-continuity-planning>.

2. Member Requested Research: Comprehensive Business Continuity Program. (2011). Available to members of the Security Executive Council, <www.securityexecutivecouncil.com>.

3. 2008 Continuity Insights and KPMG Advisory Services Business Continuity Management Benchmarking Report. (2008). *Continuity Insights* magazine and KPMG LLP. Available from <http://www.continuityinsights.com/sites/continuityinsights.com/files/legacyfiles/CI-KPMG08-FinalResults.pdf>.

4. Canadian Small Business Owners Vulnerable to Everyday Risks. (October 20, 2009). *Bloomberg*. <http://www.bloomberg.com/apps/news?pid=newsarchive&sid=aRC1XGQ2kU.M>.

5. Z1600-08: Emergency Management and Business Continuity Programs. (August, 2008). Canadian Standards Association. Available from <http://shop.csa.ca/en/canada/injury-prevention/z1600-08/invt/27028572008/>.

6. ASIS International. (2005). *Business Continuity Guideline: A Practical Approach for Emergency Preparedness, Crisis Management, and Disaster Recovery*. Available from <https://www.asisonline.org/Standards-Guidelines/Guidelines/published/Pages/Business-Continuity-Guideline_A-Practical-Approach-for-Emergency-Preparedness_Crisis-Management_and-Disaster-Recovery.aspx?cart = f2d3129ef48d4cd98550605f5193b4d5>.

7. Emergency Management Planning Guide 2010–2011. (2010). Public Safety Canada. Available from <http://www.publicsafety.gc.ca/prg/em/emp/emp-2010-11-eng.aspx>.

8. NFPA 1600 Standard on Disaster/Emergency Management and Business Continuity Programs. (2007). National Fire Protection Association (NFPA). Available from <http://www.nfpa.org/assets/files/pdf/nfpa1600.pdf>.

9. Walker, S., & Brennan, J. (2010). *Security Careers: Defining Jobs, Compensation, Qualifications* (2nd ed.). Available to members of the Security Executive Council, <www.securityexecutivecouncil.com>.

About Contributing Editor Dean Correia

Dean Correia, contributing editor of the *Business Continuity* playbook, has had a career in operations and loss prevention in Canada spanning more than 20 years, holding senior leadership roles with global brands GAP, Starbucks Coffee, and Walmart. Dean is skilled at influencing stakeholders to embed an enduring legacy through process improvements and the creation of sustainable programs that contribute profit and add value through the protection of people and securing of assets.

Dean is a Certified Protection Professional (CPP) and licensed private investigator whose other certifications include handwriting content analysis, interview/interrogation, and executive protection. An experienced workshop facilitator and passionate public speaker globally, Dean is an emeritus faculty member of the Security Executive Council.

Dean served a three-year term on the board of the US-based National Food Safety Security Council and has been an engaged member of the Retail Council of Canada for more than a decade, having led the national loss prevention conferences for both of these organizations in 2006 and 2008, respectively.

Some of Dean's career highlights include successfully leading Walmart Canada's security event planning for the 2010 Vancouver Olympics and the G8/G20 summit. Dean spearheaded the creation of business continuity and crisis management plans for Walmart Canada and Walmart Canada Bank. At both Walmart Canada and Starbucks Coffee, Dean played a key role in the creation, development, and implementation of auditing and investigative programs that delivered millions of dollars to the bottom line.

About the Authors

Bob Hayes has more than 25 years of experience developing security programs and providing security services for corporations, including eight years as the CSO at Georgia Pacific and nine years as security operations manager at 3M. His security experience spans the manufacturing, distribution, research and development, and consumer products industries as well as national critical infrastructure organizations. Additionally, he has more than 10 years of successful law enforcement and training experience in Florida and Michigan. Bob is a recognized innovator in the security field and was named as one of the 25 Most Influential People in the Security Industry by *Security Magazine*. He is a frequent speaker at key industry events. He is a leading expert on security issues and has been quoted by such major media outlets as the *Wall Street Journal* and *Forbes*. Bob is currently the managing director of the Security Executive Council.

Kathleen Kotwica has a PhD in experimental psychology from DePaul University and has had a career as a researcher and knowledge strategist. Her experience includes positions as information architecture consultant at a New England consulting firm, director of online research at CXO Media (IDG), and research associate at Children's Hospital in Boston. She has authored and edited security industry trade and business articles and has spoken at security-related conferences including CSO Perspectives, SecureWorld Expo, ASIS, and CSCMP. In her current role as EVP and chief knowledge strategist at the Security Executive Council she leads the development and production of Council tools, solutions, and publications. She additionally conducts industry research and analysis to improve security and risk management practices.

About Elsevier's Security Executive Council Risk Management Portfolio

Elsevier's Security Executive Council Risk Management Portfolio is the voice of the security leader. It equips executives, practitioners, and educators with research-based, proven information and practical solutions for successful security and risk management programs. This portfolio covers topics in the areas of risk mitigation and assessment, ideation and implementation, and professional development. It brings trusted operational research, risk management advice, tactics, and tools to business professionals. Previously available only to the Security Executive Council community, this content—covering corporate security, enterprise crisis management, global IT security, and more—provides real-world solutions and "how-to" applications. This portfolio enables business and security executives, security practitioners, and educators to implement new physical and digital risk management strategies and build successful security and risk management programs.

Elsevier's Security Executive Council Risk Management Portfolio is a key part of the *Elsevier Risk Management and Security Collection.* The collection provides a complete portfolio of titles for the business executive, practitioner, and educator by bringing together the best imprints in risk management, security leadership, digital forensics, IT security, physical security, homeland security, and emergency management: Syngress, which provides cutting-edge computer and information security material; Butterworth Heinemann, the premier security, risk management, homeland security, and disaster-preparedness publisher; and Anderson Publishing, a leader in criminal justice publishing for more than 40 years. These imprints, along with the addition of Security Executive Council content, bring the work of highly regarded authors into one prestigious, complete collection.

The Security Executive Council (www.securityexecutivecouncil.com) is a leading problem-solving research and services organization focused on helping businesses build value while improving their ability to effectively manage and mitigate risk. Drawing on the collective knowledge of a large community of successful security practitioners, experts, and strategic alliance partners, the Council develops strategy and insight and identifies proven practices that cannot be found anywhere else. Their research, services, and tools are focused on protecting people, brand, information, physical assets, and the bottom line.

Elsevier (www.elsevier.com) is an international multimedia publishing company that provides world-class information and innovative solutions tools. It is part of Reed Elsevier, a world-leading provider of professional information solutions in the science, medical, risk, legal, and business sectors.

Industry Applicability Validation

Industry applicability validation was performed by:

Silvia Fraser, Supervisor, Business Strategies and Risk Management Office, Corporate Security, City of Toronto
Rick Gipson, Manager, Corporate Security, Koch Industries, Inc.
Radford Jones, Emeritus Faculty, Security Executive Council
Bob Marentette, Director of Corporate Security, Art Gallery of Hamilton, Ontario
Jerome Miller, Emeritus Faculty, Security Executive Council
Alain Normand, Manager, Emergency Measures, The Corporation of the City of Brampton, Ontario

Printed and bound by CPI Group (UK) Ltd, Croydon, CR0 4YY

08/05/2025

01864876-0001